Text

Carl Henrik Langebaek

Photographs:

Jorge Mario Múnera
Christian Zitzmann
Juan Pablo Gnecco
Patrick Rouillard

Design and Layout:

L Santiago Correa L.

Clay Models:

Cecilia Vargas

Colaboration:

Museo del Oro - Banco de la República

Compiling, Editing, Printing and Binding:

Compañía Litográfica Nacional S.A.
Editorial Colina

Text Composition and Color Selection:

Fotolito Colina

Distribution:

Hola Colina Ltda.
Telephone: 266 32 11 Medellín 217 04 55 Santafé de Bogotá Apartado 3674,
Medellín, Colombia

ISBN: 958-638-052-1

GOLD and PRECOLUMBIAN CULTURES

GOLD

and PRECOLUMBIAN CULTURES

Carl Henrik Langebaek

Compañía Litográfica Nacional S.A.

1992

TABLE OF CONTENTS

Introduction

Colombia, the country of "El Dorado", is renowned for the thousands of prehispanic objects displayed in the Museo del Oro, not to mention the hundreds of discoveries unearthed annually by treasure seeking "guaqueros" all over the country. However, more than an enormous collection of valuable objects, the Gold Museum is a showcase for the rich patrimony bequeathed by cultures whose goldwork reached surprising heights. Archaeologists are not particularly interested in specific pieces on exhibit at the Museum. As a matter of fact, we consider them useful, relative to the amount of information they provide concerning the societies which produced them. That is one aspect of our work. Another is to make that knowledge available to the general public.[1]

Archaelogists approach the study of the pieces in the Museum from different perspectives. One approach consists of analyzing goldworking development, emphasizing the technological expertise of the metalsmiths. The methods employed by indigenous artisans to work metals - gold and copper being among the most important - required a certain knowledge of the minerals' malleability and strength, the temperature at which they could be smelted and the precise proportions needed to create specific alloys. In fact, metallurgy constitutes one of the areas of communal life where the experience accumulated over generations blends, to be succeeded by stages of regular technological development. By analyzing how the pieces in the Museum were made, archaeologists gain vital information that leads toward understanding the technological mastery of the ancient metalsmiths.

Another more recently explored approach to the Museum's collection is to focus on the cultural significance of the pieces. The gold, copper, and platinum artifacts

viewed by visitors in the showcases are not mere ornaments. They are cultural products that bear rich symbolic
meanings, associated with ancient religious practices and
political hierarchies. The pieces of metal frequently
reproduce a wide range of iconography, linked to
religious specialists or shamans. The luster, smell, and
color of the metals have long been appreciated for their
attributes of facilitating hallucinatory visions. The diverse
zoomorphic figures found in precolumbian gold pieces
symbolized a clearly defined group of sacred animals and,
therefore, carried specific cultural messages.

Another way to approach prehispanic goldwork, and
this is the one we have chosen, is that of looking at its
historic development within the broadest context of social
evolution. An analysis of goldworking practices is founded
on two suppositions: firstly, it must be remembered that
the articles produced by the goldsmiths were intimately
associated with the activities of specialized political and
religious leaders, who came into being only after the
establishment of complex societies, during the last stages
of prehispanic development. The second premise is that
metal work can only attain truly significant dimensions,
such as occurred in prehispanic Colombia, when populations are capable of sustaining specialists who dedicate
their creative efforts to that activity. To be a skilled
goldsmith not only requires extraordinary ability but also
a long period of apprenticeship. The work demands
technical knowledge and an efficient and complex work
scheme for mining and smelting metals, manufacturing
molds and mass producing pieces.3

The history of prehispanic goldwork is, without a
doubt, the result of the political and economic development of the indigenous societies. Based on this premise,
we wish to describe the development and cultural context
of goldwork in the following order: firstly, by delving into
the technological and cultural aspects of working metals.
In this area the intimate relationship between the elite,
comprised of chieftains and shamans, and goldwork, will
be made perfectly clear, as well as the level of knowledge
that ancient goldsmiths mastered. Then, we shall begin
to ask ourselves how it was that these specialists came
into being and what were the primary manifestations of
those processes in the different regions of Colombia.

Cultural aspects of prehispanic goldworking

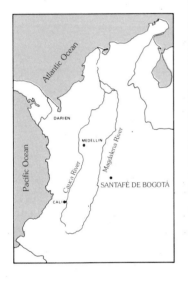

Prior to the Spanish conquest, in the territory that comprises present-day Colombia, one constant held true for all goldwork, no matter the region or era under discussion, little admiration was given to the metal itself. Relatively abundant in the country, the metals acquired considerable value only after they had been transformed into finished objects. The chronicler, López de Gomara, describes the incredulousness of Panquiaco - the son of one of the most important chieftains of the Darién region - when the Spaniards melted down indigenous gold pieces. According to Gomara, Panquiaco exclaimed:

"If I had known, Christians, that you would fight over my gold, I would not have given it to you, for I am a friend of peace and harmony. I am astounded at your blindness and insanity, that you destroy beautifully wrought pieces to make toothpicks of them and, being such good friends, you quarrel over something so insignificant and vile."

Although in some parts of the country metalsmiths created tools such as punches, chisels, hatchets, needles, and fishhooks, the fundamental use of the metals was for objects that were appreciated for their symbolic content and the messages they conveyed. Figurines representing mythical beings, were frequently used as offerings. Moreover, metal was often used to manufacture receptacles for narcotic drugs, as well as masks and diadems that symbolized political rank and power for the persons who wore them. Thus, metals were valued for their culturally accepted properties. Characteristics such as color, smell, shine and timbre proved ideal for representing cultural symbols.

Next page:
Popuro, vessel for storing lime, used when chewing coca leaves.

Unfortunately, there are very few documents that describe the lifestyle of prehispanic metalsmiths.One Spanish document refers to the Muisca population of Lenguazaque. According to the information provided by indigenous witnesses, there were at least two classes of goldworkers on the high plains of the Departments of Cundinamarca and Boyacá. Some labored producing body ornaments. Others lived apart in sanctuaries, having specialized in creating articles to be offered to the gods. In both cases, they were highly respected members of society, whose position and tools were passed down generation after generation, from father to son.The document of Lenguazaque suggests that in the most complex societies goldworking was different from the work performed by chieftains and also in many cases, from that of the shamans. However, there is no doubt

Urn from the Sierra Nevada de Santa Marta. Gold objects are frequently depicted on ceramic vessels as adornments for chieftains and shamans.

that in other societies chiefs and shamans were involved in goldwork production. The former were in charge of organizing production, particularly when raw materials had to be procured from outside sources. When this occurred, in fact, chiefs were held accountable for supplying goldworkers with materials and for storing surpluses and, later, for trading the finished pieces. Shamans, on the other hand, were responsible for deciding what type of articles should be produced. The populace would go to the shamans' sanctuaries and solicit their oracular and curative services. After ingesting narcotic drugs, particularly tobacco, the shamans would determine what type of figure the goldsmiths should craft and where it should be offered. Thus, the relationship between the goldworkers, shamans, and chieftains, was mutually complementary.

Calima nose ring. Ornament used during civil and religious ceremonies.

Technological Aspects of Prehispanic Goldworking

Enormous amounts of gold have been mined from Colombia's Central and Western Cordilleras and from the waters of the rivers that descend from those mountains, as well as from some of the rivers of the Sierra Nevada de Santa Marta and Guainía. Spanish chroniclers described two indigenous techniques for mining gold. The most common was to search for gold in alluvial deposits. There were other less frequent mentions of true mining practices, with excavations in deep shafts.

Alluvial gold was obtained in the drier months, after the high waters of the rainy winter months had exposed the surface of the gold deposits and the waters were moving more slowly so that nuggets were shaken loose from the formations and deposited in the river beds. Deep shaft mining was carried out in the western part of the country. According to descriptions by Enrique Uribe White, a Colombian engineer of English descent who visited the Remedios mines in Antioquia, there was

Etching: Indians smelting gold

evidence, even in Republican times, of ancient simple mine shafts, presumably prehispanic, that were 27 meters deep but possessed no lateral chambers or ventilation systems. Codazzi, the famous precursor of geographic surveys in Colombia, refers to the discovery of mine shafts, as well as mining instruments, in a cooper mine in the Marmato region of the Department of Caldas.

In addition to gold, Colombian Indians smelted copper and platinum. Some groups from the high plains of the Departments of Cundinamarca and Boyacá and the Cesar River valley mined copper. Usually, this metal was fused with gold to make an alloy known as tumbaga, or Guanin gold. Some of the societies, such as the Muisca, sought to refine alloys with an extremely high copper content. Copper is a metal that, in our opinion, is less valuable than gold. However, in prehispanic times, copper was much appreciated. In fact, it is more difficult to mine than gold, since systematic mining production implies an extraordinary degree of technological achievement.

In addition to the metallurgy of copper and gold, metalsmiths from some of the western sections of the country worked platinum. Indigenous technology was not sufficiently advanced to produce objects from nuggets of pure platinum, due to its extremely high fusion point.

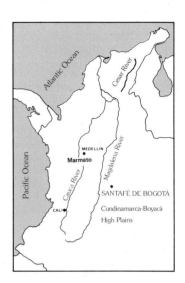

A description by Girolamo Penzoni in 1565 of how prehispanic goldworkers used blowpipes, hammers and anvils.

However, all along the Pacific coast, some quantities of platinum have been found mixed with grains of gold and are easily smelted. On exposing these grains of metal to a certain temperature, the gold melts and becomes liquid, easing the fusion of the residual platinum grains. The appearance of the finished object is, depending on the proportion of platinum, very different from that of pure gold. In Tumaco, in the extreme southwestern part of the country, as well as in various other sites along the Pacific coast, pieces have been discovered which were cast using this technique. Similar objects have been reported from the high plains of Nariño.

Until now we have discussed mining and smelting practices. These were, of course, the first phases of metallurgy. Later, diverse techniques were developed that made it possible to shape the metals. One commonly used technique for working high quality gold was to take advantage of its malleability and hammer it. By using anvils and stone hammers the early goldsmiths pounded the metal into thin sheets or fine wires. Tumbaga or copper pieces become gradually harder as they are hammered. Hardness is most appropriate for tools, but it complicates matters when producing other types of objects. The solution to this particular problem consists of exposing the objects to heat until the metal turns red hot. As successive stages of heating and hammering take place, the metal can be worked until it conforms to the desired shape.

In addition to hammering, another widely used technique employed to produce metallic objects was casting using the lost wax process. This consisted of crafting figures out of beeswax, no then covering the figure with a mixture of clay and coal dust. An opening was left in the mold into which the liquid metal could later be poured and from which the wax and gases could escape. When the mold dried, the original wax figure would have melted from being exposed to heat and the gold or alloy could then be poured into the resultant mold. Molten metal would fill the cavity and acquire the shape of the original wax mold. In some archaeologocal areas, such as Muisca and Tairona, natives had learned how to craft stone and ceramic molds by using the lost wax process and cast hundreds of identical copies from a single original.

The last stage of production for gold ornaments is finishing. Burnishing and embossing are described as usual

Stick from Calimo Poporo cast using the lost wax process.

finishing techniques, but indubitably the most important of all was forced oxidation. This technique was used on pieces made of tumbaga. Prehispanic metalsmiths learned that smelting gold and copper in certain proportions had the tremendous advantage of lowering the fusion point, a mastery that provided enormous savings of both time and materials. This is not of extreme importance when discussing the production of a few, hand-wrought pieces but it can be a critical factor when the idea is to smelt a great number of objects. Metalsmiths learned to produce pieces which had the characteristics of smell and, to a certain extent, the hardness of copper, but with high gold content. They would take advantage of the gold when it was time to burnish the surface of the pieces. Normally, objects that they wanted to make look like gold were subjected to high temperatures while encased in a mixture of tightly packed clay, salt, and certain plants. This process caused the metals that oxidized easily to remove themselves from the surface. Gold, a metal which does not readily oxidize, would remain on the surface, giving the piece the shine and light reflecting quality of pure gold.

Tairona nose ring, surface gold brought out through oxidation.

Smelting, as well as the later stages of metal working, implied specific technological developments. Hornillos, smelting pots, were among the most significant of the tools required for working gold. These ceramic receptacles - extraordinarily resistant to extreme temperature changes, poor heat conductors and reducers - limited the formation of adherents during the smelting process. Ovens to smelt metals or fragments of ovens have been discovered in the Quimbaya region, the Central Cordillera and San Agustín. Smelting fires were made hot by using ceramic blow pipes that measured 10 to 30 centimeters in length. Examples of these blow pipes have been found in the Muisca sites of Guatavita, Pasca and Sopó.

Other tools associated with working metals include spatulas, chisels, and burnishers, employed to work both wax and gold. Generally, the alloys for these tools were proportionalety high in copper and their edges, as we mentioned earlier, were hardened by hammering. The hardness of the edges and blades was sufficient for working sheets of pure gold and for crafting helmets and masks.

The Origins and Development of Goldworking Societies

SUMMARY

HUNTING/GATHERING STAGE

10,000 to 5000 B.C.
Hunters - Gatherers
Groups of relatives
Egalitarian societies

THE BEGINNINGS OF ROOT CROP AGRICULTURE

5000 B.C.
Pleistocene ends, sea level rises, and temperatures rise. Coastal populations of hunters/gatherers start to exploit resources found in swamps and mangroves. Manioc is used with ever increasing frequency and intensity. Greater emphasis on sedentary ways of life.

THE BEGINNINGS OF MAIZE AGRICULTURE

500 B.C.
Increased population, experimentation with new plants. The beginning of intensive cultivation of maize which allowed areas far removed from coasts and river banks to be dominated. Social inequalities emerge. Incipient goldworking.

Thus far, we have outlined some of the principal techniques mastered by prehispanic goldworkers and certain aspects concerning what the metal objects signified to those communities. It is important to remember, as a central and fundamental idea, that goldworking practices implied a social function determined by an evidently hierarchical aspect of communal life. Another important consideration is that goldworking refers to an activity which, in Colombia, reached levels of surprising technological complexity.

Now, we shall start to reconstruct the historic developments that allowed the goldworking specialists to develop their talents, and the chieftains and shamans to use the ornaments which those specialists produced.[4]

Between approximately 10,000 and 5000 B.C., the societies that occupied Colombian territory sustained their economy by hunting, fishing, and gathering. These societies were comprised of groups of extended families, highly specialized in hunting large animals and in taking advantage of the natural harvest of fruits and seeds available from these extensive lands. Initially, an important part of their activities consisted of hunting mastodons and primitive wild horses. Then, perhaps due to changes in climate or excessive hunting, these animals became extinct and the early inhabitants were forced to alter their hunting practices and pursue smaller prey primarily deer, rabbits, tapirs, and rodents.

When discussing the hunting/gathering stage, we refer to an extremely lengthy period during which societies were basically egalitarian. In all probability no individual members of those societies held permanent political or religious positions. The community acted on the basis of consensus, although some individual members, expert hunters or ancients, in all likelihood, held some sway over the decisions of the rest of the group. We are speaking, as a rule, of groups that practiced rigorous population control so that the size of the community would not outstrip available resources. During this period, in fact, the population behaved fundamentally as another predator, that is, a supremely efficient predator - one which took advantage of the resources nature provided by utilizing a relatively rudimentary set of stone, wood, or bone tools.

Arrowheads for hunting, scrapers for carving up prey, awls, punches, and hammers, are among the most common artifacts to have been discovered.

The panorama of the hunter/gatherer began to gradually change some 7,000 years ago. The most compelling transformation was a change from a predatory economy to economies based or agricultura, ducto the domestication of crops and animals. How the change from one type of economy to another took place is the topic of lively discussion. What is certain, is that for farming to have replaced gathering, there must have been a shift in climatic, demographic, and technological factors which acted joinltly to create a different set of conditions.

As a matter of fact, the last ice age drew to a close some 7,000 years ago. The most relevant characteristics of that period were dramatically low temperatures and the concentration of enormous quantities of ice at the polar caps. The shoreline was one of the areas of the country most sensitive to these changes. There, the water level of the seas gradually increased, average temperatures climbed and the climate turned drier. This caused many of the coastal lands and tidal basins to be invaded by swampy mangroves, a recource that offered new possibilities to human societies.

The thick growth of mangroves creates a complex ecosystem capable of offering abundant quantities of food. The leaves, on falling to the sea and decomposing through bacterial activity, are a food source that attracts a multitude of small fishes and mollusks. At the same time, the presence of these small species provides suitable conditions for abundant quantities of larger fish and birds, and naturally, man. The resources, furnished by the stands of mangrove, were so abundant that they helped some hunting/gathering societies establish more permanent settlements. Enormous accumulations of seashells, bird and animal bones, called "Concheros" in the vernacular, supply evidence of the huge interest some groups had in taking advantage of these resources created on some parts of the coast by climatic changes.

The fauna attracted by the mangrove furnished man with abundant protein, but not wild a balanced diet. The principal nutritional categories absent in these resources, such as calories, are plentiful in plants. Perhaps,this was the reason behind the coastal populations' increased consumption of vegetable resources, particularly manioc. This root crop's extraordinary resistance to drought and the ease with which large harvests can be reaped even from poor soils, presented tremendous advantages to the population. Cultivating manioc was further favored because it did not require complex systems of labor organization. Manioc, an integral part of root agriculture, implied little investment of time or labor.

One of the most relevant characteristics of this incipient agricultural process is that, for the first time, man could directly influence the biological processes of the plants and enhance production. In Concheros, or areas where remains indicate interest in the practices of gathering resources associated with the mangrove, remains of hoes as well as hatchets and scrapers have been found. Used for planting and harvesting manioc initially the tools were made of seashells, and eventually pottery. Was introduced ceramic pieces usually appeared in the shape of baking pans or large circular plates with raised borders, in which they prepared manioc bread.

The development of root crop agriculture implied, in the first instance, different food resources and increased opportunities for developing a sedentary lifestyle. The most important consequences of these new circumstances were larger populations and unaccustomed demographic and nutritional pressures, which in turn led to experimentation with novel domesticates, including corn. We now recognize that although it was probably domesticated in Mexico, maize was known in Colombia ever since the late stages of root agriculture and even in the times dominated by hunters and gatherers. For centuries, perhaps even millenia, corn complemented the diet of the indigenous populations, but that use did not lead to a specific interest in the intensive cultivation of the staple. The reasons are obvious. Corn requires an enormous amount of labor during all phases of cultivation: at planting as well as during progressive growth stages - to control weeds - and finally at harvest. Additionally, it is very sensitive to drought, and its production depends on the quality of the soil in which it is planted. The poor soil first used by early agriculturists for manioc would not have produced large maize harvests.

Paradoxically, the conditions generated by planting root crops fulfilled the prerequisites necessary for the development of maize agriculture. In the first place, population had increased and corn can feed many more people per acre than manioc. In the second place, manioc had allowed the people to establish fairly sedentary lifestyles in areas far removed from the original centers of domestication, on occasion, areas that were extremely fertile, much better suited to corn than root crops.

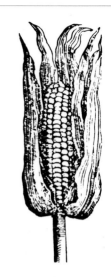

A description of indigenous agricultural practices. The domestication of food crops implied a more complicated labor system, which in turn required political and religious specialists.

Maize was adopted as a staple because specific pressure made it a better choice. For archaeologists it is still not quite clear what those pressures were. What we do know is the importance that this change had in prehispanic history. Firstly, the cultivation of corn allowed for and demanded population growth. Secondly, in contrast to manioc, it can be cultivated at considerably high altitudes. This, added to corn's requirement of fertile land, constituted a powerful stimulant for intensifying the use of mountainous regions, heretofore avoided by the most relevant root crop agriculturists. Maize started to play a fundamental role in prehispanic development. Even more important, and also in contrast to manioc, corn has set periods for planting and harvesting, which implies the need for a far more complex labor organization than that of root crop agriculture.

Thus, as corn grew in importance, we find that political organization turned more complex. Around 400 to 500 A.D., the great majority of the indigenous communities were totally transformed. The rise of hierarchically organized societies became particularly discernible. Archaeologists have designated these societies: Chiefdoms, or hierarchically, ordered societies. They were groups of extended families in which social stratification started to become apparent, and where local villages formed confederations with dominion over a determined territory. It is precisely in the chiefdoms or "Cacicazgos" where we find the development of permanent chiefs, and shamans.

Above all, the chiefs were responsible for organizing the system of economic production, storage, and the distribution of any surpluses. The shaman, on the other hand, was entrusted with the duty of programming agricultural tasks through the development and employment of calendars as well as by administering and controlling religious rites and practices. Both the chief and the shaman represented interests that continued to be closely linked with those of their community. Fundamentally, they comprised an elite that possessed the authority to make decisions which in the economic context affected the entire community and which required a centralized organization of labor.

The prestige of the chieftains and shamans did not specifically emanate from their person, but rather from

Next Page:
The representation of religious and civil specialists became quite commonplace in seed crop cultures. Ceramic figurine from the Sierra Nevada de Santa Marta.

their role as representatives of the interests of the respective communities. The various maize agricultural societies encountered by the Spaniards were proud of their rich and powerful chieftains and shamans, although, in the end, all of the goods that made those leaders "rich" and "powerful" continued to belong to the community, not to the individuals. The flourishing of cacicazgos assuredly coincides with the appearance in the archaeological record of evidence of social stratification. Initially, a great quantity of luxury items, presumably only for use by the elite, began to appear: necklace beads carved from semi-precious stones and gold, ceremonial staffs, body ornaments, and diadems. Furthermore, evidence exists of differential treatment of the dead, ceramic figures associated with shamanistic rituals and ceremonial structures. Simultaneously, ever increasing specialization develops: different villages start to specialize in diverse activities and with this, increased trade between regions and in some places, specialized merchants and markets.

With the advent of the cacicazgos, goldworking development receives a definitive thrust. Certainly, goldwork was known for hundreds of years prior to the development of chiefdoms, however, it is clear that mass or serial production of metallic objects appeared only with the development of maize agriculture and chiefdoms.

The progress described here, beginning with the hunting/gathering period and culminating with the development of hierarchical societies, constitutes but a brief sketch of the complex prehispanic historic processes. Certainly, not all of the phenomena described here occurred within the same time frame, in all places. A rough generalization would attest to the fact that the development of maize agriculture was particularly successful in the higher regions, while root agriculture retained some of its initial importance in many of the lowland expanses. Another particularity is that the development of chiefdoms probably occurred earlier in the southern part of the country, that is, in San Agustín, Tierradentro, Calima and adjacent areas, while northern Andean populations were not organized is chiefdoms until later. By 1300 A.D., however, the northern societies had already reached impressive levels of political sophistication. The very nature of the chiefdom political organization was not the same in the various time frames and geographical settings. In the southern part of the country the earliest recorded chiefdoms emphasized monumental statuary and the elaboration of few, but spectacular goldworks. What is most impressive about this period is the monumental quality of the works with which the different chieftains and their communities wished to proclaim their stature. Later, both in the south as well as in the north, we no longer find such a marked interest in sumptuous monumental works nor in the elaboration of unique gold or ceramic pieces. Later sociaties placed emphasis on the construction of works of agricultural infrastructure oriented toward feeding a growing population, as well as the serial production of great quantities of gold and ceramic objects, simpler and more homogeneous than those produced in earlier periods.

Before starting to describe the social and goldworking developments in the territory that comprises present day Colombia, certain points must be clarified. In the first place, we shall start this description with societies established in the south since they were the first to develop goldwork. Nariño, however, shall be discussed somewhat later because its goldworking development was different from all of the other southern cultures. Secondly, we wish to clarify that goldwork developments such as those of Urab and Guainía have not been included. Little more than limited references exist in chronicles or archive documents and there are no contemporary studies,thus it is not known what type of pieces they produced, nor how. Lastly, we shall use well-known classifications of indigenous cultural areas. This concept, has met with criticism because it assumes cultural homogeneity based on the distribution of certain types of similar ornaments. On the other hand, it should be remembered that borders for "cultural areas" were always loosely interpreted. These considerations lead toward the definition of "area" more as a geographic concept than a cultural one. We shall conserve terms such as Calima and Muisca because we believe them to be familiar to the majority of the readers.

Calima

"Canastero" Calima, Ilama phase

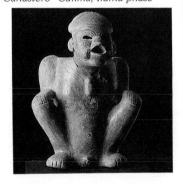

The Calima area is located in the Western Cordillera and in the central basin of the Cauca River. It is a territory which, under certain conditions of agricultural management results optimal for the production of staples and the development of maize agriculture. Today we know that human settlement in the region dates back to the fifth millennium B.C., when groups of hunters/gatherers lived in the high basin of the Dagua River. Around 1500 B.C. and until the first century of the common era, the region was occupied by societies that lived in centralized settlements and whose ceramics were characterized by incised decoration, the presence of zoomorphic and anthropomorphic receptacles, as well as receptacles known as "canasteros" or barket carriers and "patones", or big foot figures. These share certain characteristics with earlier ceramics discovered in Ecuador, some phases of the Tumaco and Jama-Coaque cultures and certain pieces discovered at sites in the lower Cauca River valley, such as Catanguero. These groups, known as Ilama, probably were already aware of maize cultivation but were not a fully developed maize agricultural society.

From the beginning of the ove era until 1100 A.D., the inhabitants of the Calima region certainly cultivated beans, arracacha - a tuber similar to sweet potato - gourds and corn. This phase known as Yotoco, is characterized by the construction of mountainside terraces, roads and house platforms, as well as enormous fields of crops with systems of parallel canals which permitted intensive agricultural development while reducing the risks of erosion. Yotoco ceramics have some similarities with Ilama pieces, although Yotoco emphasized negative painted rather than incised decoration. The Yotoco phase is characterized furthermore by the presence of pipes for smoking tobacco

"Patón" Calima, Ilama phase

SUMMARY

CALIMA

Occupation of the region in 5000 B.C.

CALIMA-ILAMA

1500 B.C. - 100 A.D.

Ceramics with incised decoration, zoomorphic vessels. Small scale cultivation of maize.

GOLDWORKING

Some hammered sheets of gold suggest elementary goldworking practices.

CALIMA-YOTOCO

100 B.C. - 1300 A.D.

Cultivation of beans, arracacha, squash and maize. Intensive agriculture. Construction of terraces, roads, and housing. Ceramics with painted negative decoration. Pipes for smoking tobacco and poporos for storing lime. Probable emergence of religious and political specialists.

GOLDWORKING

Emphasis on spectacular hammered or cast pieces.

CALIMA-SONSO

1100 - 1600 A.D.

Serial production of ceramics. Burials suggest social differentiation. Trade with neighboring areas.

GOLDWORKING

Casting using the lost wax process. Predomination of casting as opposed to hammering. Frequent use of tumbaga.

Calima-Yotoco "Alcarraza"

Sonso receptacle

Stick figurehead from a Calima-Yotoco "Poporo"

and "poporos" or receptacles for housing lime, a substance used when chewing coca leaves. These indications, added to the evidence of intensive agricultural endeavors, suggest that Yotoco constituted a period of social change during which civil and religious specialists probably evolved.

The Sonso phase began in the 12th century. This phase marked the beginning of the serial production of a type of pottery vastly different from the ceramic record of earlier periods, burials in tombs 15 or more meters deep, trade activities that supplied the region with seashells and the construction of artificial platforms on the sides of the mountains. The Sonso phase of the 1500's perhaps refers to the group of Indians which the Spaniards called "Gorrones".

According to documents from the end of the 1500's, the Indians from the areas surrounding Cali divided themselves into three regions. Those who occupied the lands near the Cauca River emphasized maize and cotton cultivation as well as fishing. Those in the nearby mountains raised potatoes and beans and produced ceramic pots. To the west, on the Pacific coast, the inhabitants were extremely proficient in weaving reed baskets.

Calima goldwork reached its highest splendor in the Yotoco phase, that is if the production of spectacular objects is the point of reference. Some Ilama ceramic vessels have been discovered together with hammered sheets of pure gold. However, these are isolated finds and of little significance. The Yotoco phase, to the contrary, can be described as a period of noteworthy production of hammered and cast pieces. Firstly, there is an outstanding group of pieces denominated "alfileres" - elongated pins cast from different metals which are thought to have been used for extracting lime from poporos. Likewise, mention should be made of the production of masks, pectorals and receptacles of varying types created by assembling sheets of hammered or embossed gold.

During the Sonso phase, goldwork like ceramics, demonstrated dramatic changes when compared to Yotoco examples. It would appear, that the largest quantity of pieces from the centuries immediately preceding the Spanish conquest correspond to nose rings shaped like twisted nails, small semicircular nose rings and a few heart shaped pectorals. These pieces were cast in tumbaga using the lost wax process. Summarizing, the Sonso phase marks the beginning of the use of hard alloys to

the detriment of purer gold pieces and the predominance of casting as opposed to hammering. We shall see this progression in other southern Colombia regions for later periods of occupation.

Calima-Yotoco breast plate

Tumaco

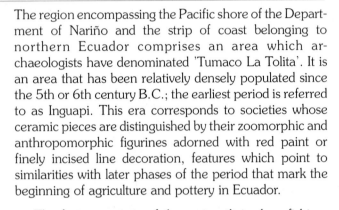

The region encompassing the Pacific shore of the Department of Nariño and the strip of coast belonging to northern Ecuador comprises an area which archaeologists have denominated 'Tumaco La Tolita'. It is an area that has been relatively densely populated since the 5th or 6th century B.C.; the earliest period is referred to as Inguapi. This era corresponds to societies whose ceramic pieces are distinguished by their zoomorphic and anthropomorphic figurines adorned with red paint or finely incised line decoration, features which point to similarities with later phases of the period that mark the beginning of agriculture and pottery in Ecuador.

The first occupants of the region thrived on fishing, gathering crabs and only secondarily from gathering mollusks, harvesting fruits and hunting. Their settlements were oriented toward dominating the abundant mangroves of the region and did not alter the landscape in any appreciable way. Later, during the period known as Bucheli, the population would modify its ceramic practices placing less emphasis on the elaboration of figurines and the use of paint. During the last phases of this population, the Indians of the Tumaco region built mounds over which they erected their dwellings. Little is known about their economy. Some data suggest that when the Spaniards arrived the political organization of the people of the region was not as complex as that of their neighbors in the Andean zone. An important part of their economic activities was directed toward supplying the population of the highlands with salt, mollusks, and seashells, products which they bartered for manufactured goods.

Tumaco goldwork development followed along lines similar to those of Calima and was very much in keeping with the socio-economic processes that fostered it. Inguapi, 5th century B.C. production is associated with fine gold wires, produced by cold hammering. Other dates associated with metallic objects are: 90 A.D. a date obtained from objects found at the Coche site near the Santiago River (La Tolita); 875 A.D. which corresponds to tumbaga objects found alongside Bucheli ceramic pieces. These dates permit archaeologists to suppose that in Tumaco the techniques used to produce complex alloys came after the utilization of hammering techniques. The finely wrought Inguapi wires contain 85.9% gold and 10.3% silver, a composition that all but duplicates local alluvial gold. Later pieces were cast from alloys of gold and copper or gold and platinum.

Anthropomorphic Tumaco figurine

SUMMARY

TUMACO-INGUAPI

500 - 400 B.C.

Economy based on fishing, cultivating fruit trees, and hunting. Settlements associated with mangroves. Emphasis on the elaboration of anthropomorphic and zoomorphic figurines.

GOLDWORKING

Elaboration of fine, pure gold wires.

TUMACO-BUCHELI

400 B.C. - ?

Construction of mounds for dwellings, exploitation of maritime resources, and agriculture. Trade with societies from the Andean region. Less emphasis on the elaboration of figurines.

GOLDWORKING

Alloys of gold, copper, and platinum. Simple nose rings are the most common objects.

San Agustín

The San Agustín region is located in the upper Magdalena River valley and is framed by the Central and Eastern Cordilleras. As the site of the most striking progression of monumental statuary, this part of Colombia has long attracted the attention of social scientists. The ethnic history of the region has been interpreted based on two different chronologies. One of them, established by Luis Duque Gómez and Julio César Cubillos, postulates the theory of continuous development separated into an Archaic period, from 3300 to 1000 B.C., a Formative period divided in two phases: (Inferior, from 1000 to 300 B.C., and Superior, from 200 B.C. to 200 A.D.), a Regional Classical period from 300 A.D. and a Recent period from 800 A.D. until the arrival of the Spaniards.   The other chronological theory was developed by Gerardo Reichel-Dolmatoff. According to this archaeologist there might have been three principal phases, marked by abrupt changes indicating the arrival of different peoples. These stages are defined as: Horqueta, the beginnings are undecipherable but it ends in 50 A.D.; Isnos, from 50 to 400 A.D., and Sombrerillos from 1400 to 1650 A.D.

The two opinions coincide on some significant points. Firstly, that the development of monumental architecture, one of the most characteristic remains of the region, corresponds to eras prior to the Spanish incursion. Duque and Cubillos place the statuary's maximum level of development within the Regional Classical period, from 300 to 800 A.D., while Reichel-Dolmatoff has determined the highest development to have occurred between 50 to 400 A.D., during the Isnos phase. Secondly, they concur that the builders of the mounds and statuary belong to population phases associated with an era during which the local economy was heavily dependent upon the cultivation of maize.

An initial period of maize cultivation would have placed enormous emphasis on 'monumentality', then later, in the last few centuries prior to the conquest, emphasis would have shifted to the serial production of more commonplace objects.

Goldworking development follows along these same lines. In various parts of the region, hammered gold tubular and round necklace beads, diadems, wires, nose ornaments, gold rings with stone beads, "H" shaped diadems and gold covered seashells have been discovered throughout the region in association mound burials. These objects, which correspond to the statuary development, reflect ties with Calima, southern Imabaya and Tolima goldwork developments. On the other hand, the discovery of smelted drops of gold and fragments of golden sun rays in addition to the presence of alluvial gold in the regions's rivers - particularly Manzanares and Sombrerillos - point to the local production of those metallic objects.

SUMMARY

SAN AGUSTIN

3300 B.C. - 1600 A.D.

Various interpretations regarding its chronology agree that there was an early period which emphasized 'monumentality': statues, roads, and mounds. During this period spectacular gold pieces were produced. Economy was based on maize.Later occupations placed less emphasis on monumental structures. Serial production of less complicated articles.

Funerary Shrine on Mesita A in the San Agustín Archaeological Park.

Shell cover, probably discovered in San Agustín

The last phase of San Agustín goldworking is poorly documented. However, the few existing references suggest the elaboration of tumbaga nose rings. In other words, once again the large, spectacular hammered gold pieces disappear, being replaced by the production of large quantities of smaller objects, using the lost wax process.

Zoomorphic gold figure, excavated at Mesita B in the San Agustín Archaeological Park.

Tierradentro

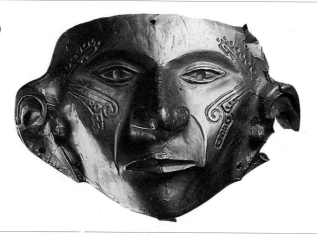

The Tierradentro region is located in the watershed areas of the Paez and Negro Rivers, tributaries of the Magdalena. Overlooking these hollows stand the permanent snow-capped mountainsides of the Nevados del Huila and Puracé. In archaeological terms it is not a very well documented territory. Without a doubt, its great attraction continues to be the existence of groups of enormous hypogea carved in the hardened volcanic ash, prevalent in areas such as Alto de San Andrés, Alto del Duende, Loma del Aguacate, and Loma Segovia.

Isolated discoveries, with no cultural association or tie to other dates, suggest that much like San Agustin, the region could have been occupied by groups of cultivators hundred of years before the ove era. To date, however, the best known data correspond to relatively recent times. A primary burial site in Santa Rosa dates back to 630 A.D. Another available date 830 A.D. corresponds to hypogea from Loma del Aguacate. However, ceramic

Pectoral discovered in Tierradentro

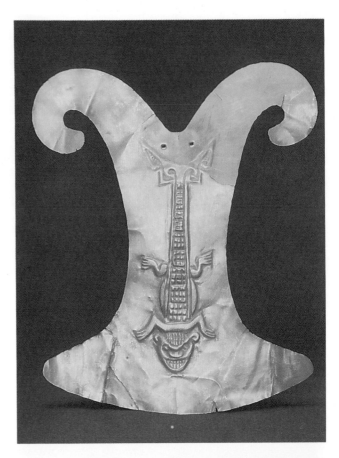

vessels similar to those from the Yotoco phase of the Calima culture and the Horqueta phase of San Agustín have been discovered in Tierradentro. It is also worth noting that there is evidence in the region indicating the existence of statuary. Following the same pattern of development as San Agustín, the statuary of Tierradentro, although less elaborate, is associated with structures built for ceremonial purposes, but apparently it is not related to the famous hypogea which were erected later.

The people who inhabited Tierradentro lived in huts constructed on terraces on the sides of the mountains. Fifteen dwelling terraces have been found on the hills of Patucue. Fragments of vessels very similar to those discovered at primary burial sites and hypogea have been encountered inside some of those dwellings. This evidence tells of the existence of life in small villages. As archaeological documentation also indicates, these groups of people cultivated maize, tomatoes, and squash, and practiced the supplementary economic activities of hunting and fishing.

According to recent studies, it is certain that Tierradentro was an important salt producing center. Near the Ullocos river and the town of Segovia, a prehispanic field was excavated; data found there confirm it as a site where waste materials associated with the exploitation of saltwater wells were discarded. The inhabitants of the region, like those from other parts of the country, evaporated saltwater in ceramic vessels that they would then break to free the blocks of compacted salt. Other activities that contributed to the local economy and which allow the archaeological record to be reconstructed, were the spinning and weaving of cotton and, tentatively, goldworking.

We would like to point out that the goldworking practices of Tierradentro seem parallel to those of San Agustín, although finds have been rare. Initially there is an arm bracelet which meets the following description: made of hammered gold with decorative designs that recall the features of the statuary found in San Agustín; and a mask from Inzá representing a face with a fanged feline mouth, which also closely resembles San Agustín iconography. Once again we find early chiefdoms emphasizing the production of hammered gold pieces, very much like those described earlier as coming from Calima, Tumaco, and San Agustín.

SUMMARY

TIERRADENTRO

? - 1600 A.D.

Little is known about its chronology. During later periods: villages on mountainsides; economy based on the cultivation of maize, tomato, and squash. Importance of local salt production.

GOLDWORKING

Some of the pieces found are similar to those of San Agustín and Calima-Yotoco. During later eras, tumbaga nose rings are produced.

Cauca

SUMMARY

CAUCA

? - 1600 A.D.

Remains of monumental statuary and architecture, whose chronology is not certain. In later epochs, economy based on the cultivation of maize, potatoes, and avocados.

GOLDWORKING

Later goldwork is characterized by its emphasis on tumbaga, casting in the lost wax process, and the elaboration of pendants in bird shapes and simple nose rings.

In the upper Cauca River basin and the areas surrounding Popayán, rather isolated evidence has been found of prehispanic development. These include remains of statuary, etchings in stone and even some manifestations of monumental statuary. The archaeological panorama for the later periods of this region is relatively clear. However, in contrast to San Agustín, Calima and Tumaco, it is very difficult to reconstruct the history of the earliest developments of the region, even in general terms, or to decipher patterns that could be used for comparison to neighboring areas.

In later eras, the predominating regional ceramic tradition concentrated on the serial production of vessels very similar to those from the Sonso phase of Calima. The local economy was based on the cultivation of maize, potatoes, and avocados. It is known, furthermore, that the people of the region participated in marketing networks, trading goods with other regions. From the Pacific coast, they obtained seashells and probably salt. From the Andes of Antioquia, they procured tumbaga nose rings. According to available data, the metal pieces discovered so far correspond to later occupations. Cauca goldwork is principally known for two kinds of figures. The most chacteristic are bird-shaped pendants, generally made of tumbaga cast in the lost wax process. The other series of pieces are nose rings shaped like twisted nails. Clearly in both cases, they are objects similar to those goldworkers created in northern Colombia between 500 and 1500 A.D.

Cauca pendant

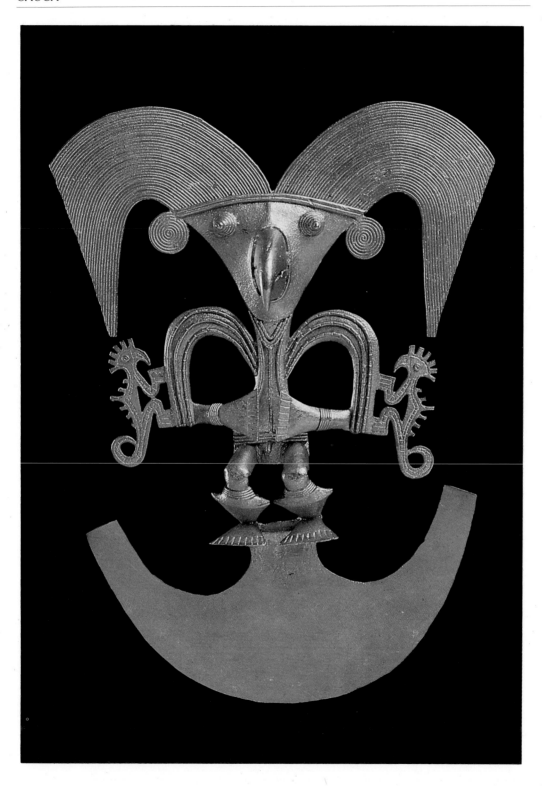

Tolima

Tolima breast plate terminating in half moon at the bottom. Similar although much smaller pieces have been found in San Agustín.

The term 'Tolima' has been used somewhat arbitrarily to refer to a series of cultural manifestations from the southern part of the Central Cordillera and the Magdalena River valley, including sites such as Chaparral, Campohermoso, and Saldaña, in the present day Department of Tolima. As in the case of Cauca, the Tolima archaeological record is not complete. Some evidence, however, points to two periods of occupation, corresponding, in general terms, to the trends already described for other parts of southern Colombia.

The ceramic pieces excavated at Chaparral include decorated vessels with incisions, and their shapes recall the early developments of San Agustín and Calima. The goldwork found beside these ceramic pieces include ring-shaped nose ornaments, anthropo-zoomorphic pendants ending in half moon shapes, necklace beads, geometric abstractions of the human figure, pendants in the shape of birds and depilating tweezers. These pieces are reminiscent of developments from the Yotoco phase of Calima. In fact, some objects corresponding to the area called Tolima have been discovered in tombs beside Yotoco artifacts. By the same token, Tolima pieces with bird shaped representations and pendants ending in half moon shapes, have been discovered in tomb excavations in San Agustín.

This body of evidence points to occupation before 900 A.D. Unfortunately, there is little that can be added to this hypothesis. At Chaparral excavation sites, the discovery of "manos" and "metates", both stone grinding instruments, would indicate that in the Tolima area the earliest manifestations of goldwork are also associated with groups of maize agriculturests. There is no evidence, however, concerning demographic density or settlement patterns.

As usual, our information expands appreciably when discussing later occupations. In the 1500's, the area was occupied by Pijao Indians. These societies followed a settlement organization consisting of huts scattered over the sides of the mountains. Maize, beans, arracacha, manioc, sweet potato, and other root crops common to the colder climates are described as being among the most important products of their economy. Spanish reports suggest that hunting activities were quite important while fishing was less popular.

In general terms, two classes of Pijao groups are mentioned: those of the mountains and those of the lowlands. These latter included communities such as Coyaima and Natagaima which sustained bloody wars with the Andean Pijaos. However, both the mountain dwellers and the other Pijaos were governed by similar codes of cultural beliefs. Extended families banded together to form groups led by warrior chieftains. In times of peace, each group was independent. In case of war, diverse groups tended to form alliances under the leadership of the chief of one of the communities involved.

The ceramics and goldwork produced by later Tolima groups differ greatly from those created in earlier periods. The pottery is extremely varied. Tolima goldwork would stand out on the basis of the heart-shaped pectorals alone. These were made by smelting the metals to create the copper and gold alloy which was then cast using the lost wax process. Diverse stone carvings found in this geographic zone depict these goldwork shapes, which came to be copied in more northern areas, particularly in the Muisca region.

SUMMARY

TOLIMA

There were probably at least two periods, but archaeological evidence is scarce. During the earlier period, economy was based on the cultivation of maize. Ceramics are similar to those of Calima-Yotoco and San Agustín. During the later period, the region was occupied by Pijao Indians.

GOLDWORKING

During the earlier period, elaboration of pure gold objects: rings, pendants, and depilating tweezers. In later eras, emphasis was placed on the use of tumbaga. Production of heart-shaped pectorals.

Anthropomorphic figure.

Nariño

In contrast to other regions of southern Colombia, we have no proof at all about the ancient periods of hunting and gathering, early agriculturists, or even the precursors of intensive cultivation of maize by the Andes of Nariño. In fact, the first evidence of population in the region corresponds to surprisingly late dates, around 600 A.D., when groups that had already fully developed maize agriculture began occupying the region. As a reason for this historically late occupation, it is argued that sedentary or semi-sedentary settlements in the region were made all but impossible by frequent volcanic eruptions. Yet, paradoxically, the rich soil formed by the volcanic activity became one of the regions' principal attractions. Once the periods of the most violent eruptions had passed, the territory was invaded by foreign cultures.

These groups which arrived in the 7th century are known as Piartal-Tuza, a term associated with the ethnicity which the Spaniards called Pastos, and Capuli, and which appears to be linked to some not very satisfactorily defined group or groups. In both cases these societies probably originated in Ecuador and shared few ties with the societies of the rest of southern Colombia.

Piartal corresponds to the Pastos' first period of development. During this time, the Indians lived in centralized villages conformed of numerous huts with stamped earth floors. They developed goldworking, ceramics, and textile industries. Chronologically, we refer to a period from 600 to 1200 A.D. In all probability, they were a hierarchical society, organized chiefdoms. Some Piartal tombs, certainly, are extremely paltry, while others are characterized by abundant burial offerings, rich in gold, wood, textiles, and seashells.

Piartal-Tuza vessel

Tuza, on the other hand, is characterized by some changes in the ceramics and by increased population levels. Agricultural terracing with stone retaining walls has been reported and coincides with this increment in demographics, since such terracing would indicate the development of agricultural strategies to feed a growing population. In the 1300's, the majority of the people were concentrated in the cold high plains of Túquerres and Ipiales, as well as in the Guaitara River canyon which enjoyed more temperate climates.

Ethnohistorical data would suggest that the Pastos maintained two basic economic activities. Each community developed specific yet diverse crops at different altitudes. This agricultural strategy meant that the population could easily obtain food sources from different origins by simply travelling extraordinarily short distances. Additionally, they had a well developed network for marketing their products. The Pastos organized periodic markets for their goods and produce that attracted merchants from neighboring groups living in Ecuador. Those merchants brought their goods from as far south as the Inca Empire. In fact, in the last few years before the arrival of the Spaniards, it is conceivable that some of their economic activities were affected by the expansion of the

SUMMARY

NARIÑO PIARTAL-TUZA

600 - 1600 A.D.

Region uninhabited prior to 600 A.D., due most likely to volcanic activity. Initial Tuza occupation characterized by centralized villages and social stratification. Tuza period: increased population, agricultural terracing. Markets were developed and trade carried out with Ecuador, the Amazon region, and the Pacific coast.

GOLDWORKING

Expert handling of forced oxidation to control gold surface, creating multicolored tumbaga pieces such as Pan's pipes, bells, and applications for textiles.

NARIÑO-CAPULI

600 - 1600 A.D.

Societies that based their economy on the cultivation of maize but perhaps not as complex as the Piartal-Tuza. Ceramics with negative decoration, and coca production.

GOLDWORKING

Frequent use of pure gold. Creation of ear rings, pendants, nipple shields, and earcuffs.

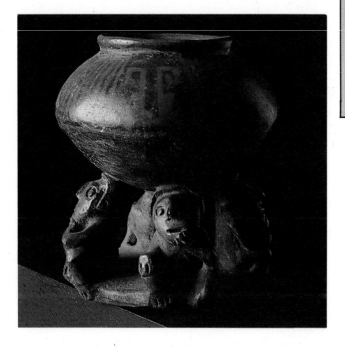

Capulí vessel

Inca Empire, whose northern frontier almost reached the present day border of Ecuador and Colombia.

The Capulí archaeological complex also reflects a society which dedicated its efforts to the cultivation of maize but which apparently did not reach the same degree of complexity as that of the Pastos. Geographically, they inhabited the Guaitara River basin. The ceramics from this period, decorated with black and red paint, are related to some material excavated in the Carchí province of Ecuador. Their famous "coqueros", seated representations of shamans chewing coca leaves, are outstanding.

The goldwork of Piartal-Tuza and Capulí differ tremendously. Nonetheless, in some cases, pieces belonging to one or another of the traditions have been found at a single burial site. The Piartal-Tuza metal work stands out for its extraordinary finish, caused by using forced oxidation techniques to bring out the gold, and scraping and burnishing, which allowed designs to form that contrast in both color and texture. These techniques, commonplace in Ecuador, reached their most brilliant heights in some tumbaga disks which exhibit rich designs in two and up to three colors, obtained by using different surface treatments. Other objects common to the Piartal-Tuza

Capulí Coquero

goldwork treasury are: Pan's pipes, spherical bells or rattles, bells, nose ornaments, applications for textiles, and hanging plaques. Capulí goldwork on the other hand, includes pendants in anthropomorphic and geometric designs with embossed decoration, as well as bird-shaped pendants, nipple shields and ear ornaments, all generally made of pure gold.

The goldwork developments of Nariño require some special commentary. Indubitably, it is clear that intensive metal work in this region is also associated with relatively complex societies. The same pattern observed for other areas is also conspicuous, in that the systematic work of hard alloys corresponds to a more highly developed society - the Pastos - while the work of pieces in purer gold corresponds to less complex groups. What is peculiar in Nariño is that, first of all, two types of technologically different goldwork traditions coexisted in the same area until the 16th century. Another interesting aspect of the region's goldwork is that as it concerns the manifestation of groups which probably arrived very late historically, it is very difficult to establish parallels with groups from other regions of Colombia.

Capulí ear pendant

Quimbaya

Anthropomorphic Quimbaya figure

Quimbaya, an ambiguous term which initially was used to designate only one of the many societies of the central basin of the Cauca River, has been employed in two ways: to describe a group of goldwork manifestations found in an area stretching from the Departments of Caldas and Risaralda to the central part of the Department of Antioquia; and to classify a series of indigenous groups from the Central Cordillera, probably related through their cultural production and traditions.

Here, by Quimbaya we shall be referring to an area between the central Cauca River valley, in the portion that is bordered by the Central Cordillera, and the Andes of the extreme southern part of the Department of Antioquia, thus including sectors of the Central as well as the Western Cordillera. We have defined it this way because, despite regional variations and although we are definitely not speaking of a community in ethnic nor cultural terms, we consider many of the historic processes to have been common to the groups of the region. With the Quimbaya area we leave the realm of the southern societies and enter the dominion of the northern part of the country.

Tentatively, we shall discuss the two periods of occupation in this region. Lamentably, we do so basing our knowledge on isolated data and on comparisons of style which await archaeological evaluation. A first stage corresponds to what has been called Quimbaya Classic. The discoveries associated with this tradition consist of incised brownware and spectacular examples of goldwork. This period, which perhaps runs from the first two centuries to the 10th century A.D., had been principally characterized in the Andean region of the Departments of Caldas, Risaralda and Quindío by the presence of ceramics and goldwork related to the Yotoco phase of Calima, San

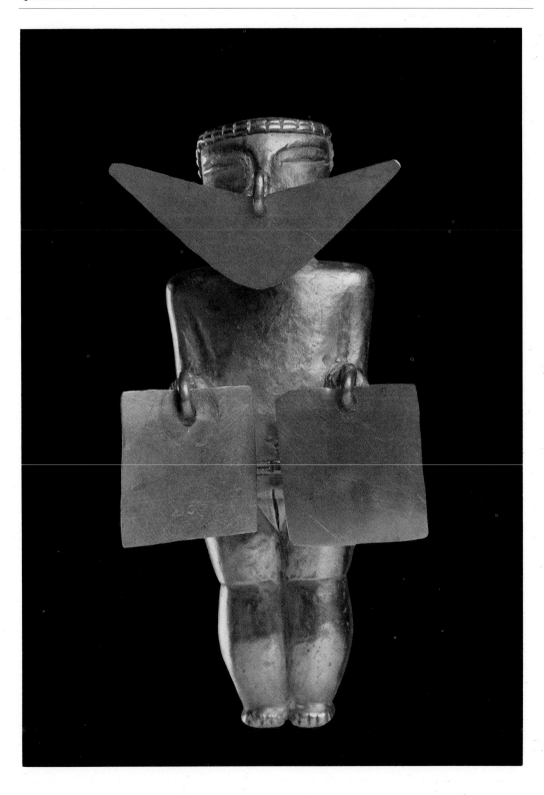

Agustín, and Tolima. Little is known about the lifestyle of these people. Simply there are no data on their population pattern, economy or level of sociopolitical complexity.

What has become clear is that beside pieces of Yotoco goldwork, we start to uncover evidence of a highly developed local metallurgy that is far removed from the traditional manifestations of southern goldworking. Their elaboration, both in pure gold and tumbaga, of anthropomorphic and fruit shaped poporos, helmets with embossed decoration, cast globular and tubular necklace beads, bird-shaped pendants, nose rings with lateral prolongations, and beads in the shape of human faces with gentle expressions are outstanding. Later on we shall describe how the goldwork of the societies from the northern part of the country progressed, essentially, by imitating these types of pieces.

In later eras, between the 10th and 16th centuries A.D., other goldworking practices developed. In the first place, one observes the diminished interest in producing extraordinary pieces, to be replaced by an intensification of the mass production of smaller objects. There were nose rings in the shape of twisted nails, and nose rings

SUMMARY

QUIMBAYA CLASSIC

200 A.D. - 1000 A.D.

Earlier period little known. To date it constitutes the earliest evidence of agricultural societies to inhabit the region of the central Cauca River Valley and Antioquia. Incised brownware, and occasionally ceramics similar to those of Calima-Yotoco belong to this period.

GOLDWORKING

Casting in the lost wax process, in pure gold or tumbaga, of poporos, nose rings, and necklace beads.

LATE QUIMBAYA

1000 - 1600 A.D.

Great variety in ceramic traditions. The existence of small autonomous communities whose economy is based on maize agriculture. Trade networks established with the Caribbean coast, Magdalena Valley, and the southern part of the country.

GOLDWORKING

Serial production of articles such as nose rings. Emphasis on tumbaga. Dabeiba becomes a specialized goldworking center.

Classical Quimbaya Poporo

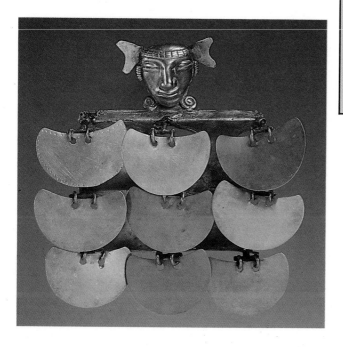

Classical Quimbaya Pectoral

Anthropomorphic ceramic figure,
Late Quimbaya (900 to 1500 A.D.)

and flat circular pendants with raised decoration. In the 16th century, the Andean mountains of the Department of Antioquia were known for the voluminous production of these articles as well as the intense mining of alluvial gold. Dabeiba, a chiefdom which specialized in goldwork practices, traded part of their production with groups from the Caribbean coast, the Magdalena River and the southern part of the country.

The ceramics associated with the later groups are extremely varied. In the south, some of the features seem to indicate similarities with the Sonso phase of Calima. Further north they developed other traditions, characterized in some cases by excised decoration and in others by incised or tricolor decorations in red, white, and black. The tremendous variety in ceramics, whose exact regional distributions and chronological developments are still being studied, coincides with great political decentralization. In the 16th century, more than eighty important chieftains were mentioned as existing in the south. The Spaniards referred to the regional communities as groups of friends and relatives who consolidated when war occurred. In the north, the societies of Antioquia were organized in "parcialidades" (partialities), also independent among themselves. The economy of all these communities was based on the cultivation of maize complemented by a great textile activity, the exploitation of saltwater and gold mining.

Late Quimbaya embossed
circular plaque

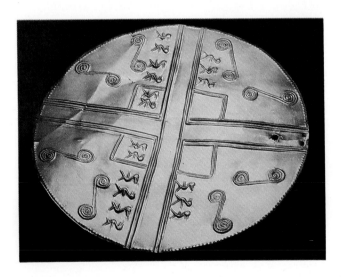

Sinú

During the first thousand years of our era, at the height of the introduction of maize agriculture in other parts of the country, the area of the lower San Jorge River and vast neighboring zones were inhabited by societies that cultivated root crops and lived in centralized villages, built on platforms near the numerous rivers and pools of the region. The people of this period of occupation cleared more than 200,000 acres of land to cultivate manioc. By constructing canals and ridges, they were able to regulate the flow of water in periods of both drought and flooding. In other words, the history of these communities is one of extraordinary technical development, associated with root-crop horticulture. However, even though later than in other places, here too maize agriculture eventually replaced the intensive cultivation of manioc, favoring profound changes in their lifestyle.

The early dense occupation of the region, associated with the construction of canals and ridges, is linked to groups that produced incised ceramics and manufactured pieces of goldwork which imitated designs and techniques from Quimbaya Classic. Although it would be presumptuous to assume that the enormous territory containing agricultural infrastructure was completely under cultivation at a given time, it would seem reasonable to presume that these societies were relatively complex, capable of deploying an abundant work force for agricultural purposes. This would imply a centralized organization of the labor force, and, therefore, the existence of civil specialists. This seems ratified, certainly, by the existence of enormous funerary mounds equipped with rich burial

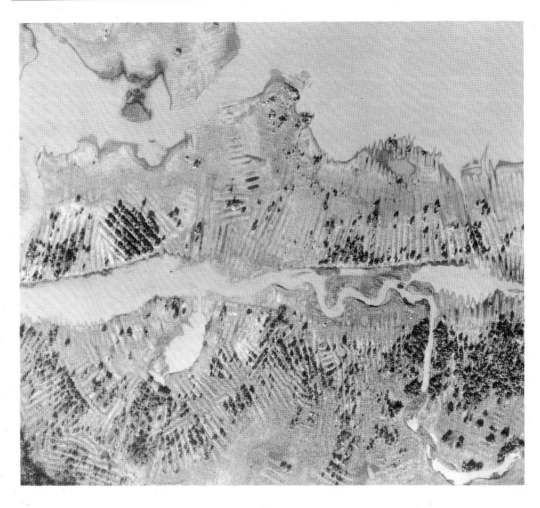

System of furrows on the lower San Jorge River.

offerings that denote important hierarchies, and by the widespread diffusion of figurines representing political and religious leaders.

In periods following 900 A.D., the area of the lower Magdalena was occupied by diverse societies classified as Malibú. They were groups of maize agriculturists each of which conserved their political independence, except in times of war,when military leaders assumed political control. Little is known of the relationship between these groups, and the occupation prior to their existence. Some authors are inclined to believe that they were "invaders", but even if this is true, we still have no knowledge concerning the pressures and conditions that led to population movements.

Anthropomorphic Sinú figure

SUMMARY

SINU CLASSIC

? - 1000 A.D.

Occupation by root crop agricultural societies. Construction of villages near rivers. Canals and ridges regulated water supply. Centralized political organization.

GOLDWORKING

Objects similar to those of the Quimbaya Classic tradition were cast using the lost wax process.

LATE SINU

1000 - 1600 A.D.

Greater emphasis on maize rather than root agriculture. Development of specialized artisans. Specialized places for producing salt, goldwork and, textiles. Firhing was also an im portant activity.

GOLDWORKING

Emphasis on casting articles using the lost wax process. Greater utilization of tumbaga than pure gold.

When the Spaniards arrived, the northern part of Colombia was characterized by a notable development of regional specialization in craft production. The Malibú, in addition to intensely cultivating maize, dedicated an important part of their time to hunting and fishing. The areas surrounding the population of Mompós were well known for cotton, abundant fishing, and goldworking. The natives of Galerazamba, north of Cartagena, were famed for the production of salt and fish, while San Jacinto specialized in textiles.

Sinú goldworking from the early periods corresponds, as has already been noted, to developments similar to those of Quimbaya Classic. The Sinú produced pure gold decorative figures as staff ends, pectorals, nose rings, and representations of animals with raised tails, which denote ties to the societies of the Andes of Antioquia, Urabá, and

Figure from the Caribbean

Central America. Later, the elaboration of tumbaga staff ends would be their predominant goldworking activity, particularly in the lower Magdalena River Valley. Mompós, for its part, had specialized in casting tumbaga nose rings and ear ornaments. Once again, as in the south, the manufacture of large quantities of objects replaces the production of few, but spectacular, pieces. The difference, however, is that for the Sinú, as in the northern part of the country in general, we are referring to late goldwork developments, which from their outset included knowledge of techniques for casting with the lost wax process and smelting complex alloys.

Decorative staff end.

Necklace beads. Representation of an animal with a raised tail, common among early goldwork from northern Colombia.

Sinú Bird staff end.

Sinú pendant.

Tairona

Neguanje incised vessel.

To the northeast of the lower Magdalena Valley, the Sierra Nevada de Santa Marta emerges to dwarf the surrounding topography. This region, as well as the neighboring coast, remained relatively marginal to historic transformations until after the advent of maize agriculture. Once the intensive cultivation of maize was incorporated into their society, the ecological potential of the region was exploited to its fullest and the Sierra became the backdrop for important social developments.

From approximately 1000 B.C. until just before our era, the coast surrounding the town of Ciénaga and especially the banks of the Toribío and Córdoba Rivers were occupied by societies that produced an incised pottery known as Malambó. According to the scant information available, the economy of these societies was based on the cultivation of root crops complemented by fishing, gathering mollusks, and hunting. We have no evidence of goldwork for this period.

The Nequanje period extended from the beginning of the Common Era until the 5th or 6th century A.D. This period marked the disappearance of Malambó incised, pottery and the appearance of the utilization of ceramic techniques found in two types of receptacles: some decorated with red paint, others with white applications and another type whose decoration was carried out using fine incisions which formed sigmoid and curvilinear motifs. More important yet, we are talking about a period during which intensive maize cultivation and goldworking practices emerged. In a pattern clearly established in other areas, the introduction or intensive maize agriculture seems to be almost catalytic in incrementing population and implementing social stratification. Nequanje corresponds, certainly, to the period during which the slopes of the Sierra started to be colonized by some of the population overflow from the coast.

Starting in the 6th century A.D., developments, both in the Sierra as well as on the neighboring coast, are credited to the period denominated Tairona, a term which in reality refers to a population from one of the sectors of the northern slopes of the Sierra. As to ceramic styles, the Tairona period marks the disappearance of painted decoration and incised curvilinear designs, characteristic of Nequanje. However, some pottery shapes continue to be fundamentally the same. Tairona marks the beginning of the total and intensive occupation of the Sierra by agricultural societies. Villages of stone structures, clustered together, are established and connected by the construction of systems of roads, drainage and irrigation works, as well as the highest development of the serial production of both ceramic and metallic objects.

Buritaca 2000. An example of a Tairona settlement on the Sierra Nevada of Santa Marta.

SUMMARY

TAIRONA

MALAMBO PERIOD

1000 B.C. - ?

Root agriculture societies occupied the most fertile lands. Economy complemented by fishing, hunting, and gathering mollusks. No evidence of goldworking.

NEGUANJE PERIOD

0 - 700 A.D.

Introduction of the intensive cultivation of maize, population growth, incipient goldworking activity. Initially, the strip of coast was populated. The permanent colonization of the Sierra Nevada de Santa Marta was begun around 500 A.D.

GOLDWORKING

Articles similar to those of the Quimbaya Classic tradition were cast using the lost wax process; especially anthropomorphic figures and bird-shaped pectorals.

TAIRONA CLASSIC

700 A.D. - 1600 A.D.

Colonization of the Sierra, networks of roadways, villages that specialized in ceramics, goldworking, and textiles. Trade between the coast and the Sierra. Bonda and Pociguecia emerge as important political centers.

GOLDWORKING

Bondigua evolves as a goldworking center. Serial production of tumbaga ornaments using the lost wax process and with the help of molds. Tairona pieces circulate to nearby regions and even to more distant territories.

Late ceramics from the Sierra Nevada de Santa Marta (600 A.D. to 1500 A.D.)

The Tairona lived in centralized villages, many of which were probably located in the temperate floor (900 - 1800 m) These were large villages with public areas, access roads, tiers, aqueducts and sewers with paved stone walls and floors, usually conformed of several dozen smaller units or "rings" for dwellings. Furthermore, the population maintained housing and cultivation terraces on high plateaus and at the foot of the Sierra, territories to which they moved so as to vary their diet, incorporating the great variety of crops and resources available. As a result of the enormous variations available from the coast - usually warm and dry but extremely fertile in some areas - and the Sierra - in general more humid, and colder in the higher climes - the populations which maintained their villages in one or another of the regions were involved in

Anthropomorphic Tairona pectoral

trade relationships. Fish, salt, cotton, and maize from the lowlands arrived into the hands of the Indians on the high cold lands in exchange for blankets, goldwork, and agricultural products common to those regions.

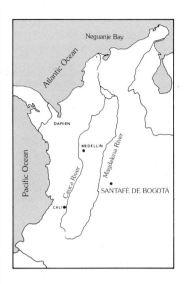

The Tairona political organization was complex. Each town was divided into "barrios", possibly areas destined for groups of relatives. Caciques or chiefs were respected as civil leaders and Nahomas were honored as religious leaders. The functions of both the civil as well as the religious leaders could be performed only after the individuals had endured rigorous training, which lasted years and demanded exhausting days of fasting and study. When the Spaniards arrived, some villages, particularly Bonda and Pocigüeica, possessed a power and prestige that was recognized over vast sections of the Sierra and the coast. Many communities continued, however, to retain their independence well into the 1500's.

The goldwork of the Sierra and neighboring regions reached its greatest splendor in the measure that those same communities adopted more and more complex economic orders. Nequanje goldwork was already characterized by the creation of anthropomorphic figures, bird-shaped pectorals or "aguilas" (eagles) and a further series of figures very much like those of Quimbaya Classic. Tairona goldwork continued to place great emphasis on casting. They increased the custom of forced oxidation to highlight the gold, and above all, they started the production of enormous quantities of pieces that represent an extraordinarily rich variety of figures in man-bird or man-bat shapes, as well as diverse representations of fauna. Some of these pieces were cast using molds which allowed them to produce numerous copies from a single original. In fact, the Tairona gold pieces deposited in the Museum number in the thousands.

Tairona goldworkers were supplied with gold mined from the Don Diego, Buritaca, and Guachica Rivers. In Bondigua, a place near the town of Bonda, as well as in some parts of the Buritaca River basin, specialized goldworking centers developed. Thousands of necklace beads, circular shaped pectorals, "eagles", half moon shaped earrings, globular rattles, bracelets, and diadems supplied the local population as well as communities from the Guajira, the Magdalena River basin, the Perij hills, and Lake Maracaibo basin.

Tairona aguila or eagle. Pieces such as this were common the the northern part of Colombia, Panama, and Costa Rica at the time of the Spanish conquest.

Muisca

The Muisca society is part of a group of maize agricultural societies which inhabilited the Eastern Cordillera around the 6th to 7th century of the our era. Other societies that completed the picture include the Chitareros and Guanes from Santander and the Laches from the Sierra Nevada de Cocuy. Previously, hundreds of years before our era, the Cordillera had been occupied by groups of root horticulturists who had based their economy on the cultivation of potatoes and other roots common to the cold highlands, the exploitation of saltwater, hunting, and fishing. With the Muisca period, once again we see many elements that we are accostumed to associating with maize agriculture: an increased number of settlements, which suggests demographic growth, and significant evidence of social stratification as well as notable goldworking developments.

In fact, the Muiscas were the most complex indigenous society encountered by the Spaniards in the territory that constitutes present day Colombia. The basic social unit incorporated "capitanías" (capitancies) or groups of relatives who lived in centralized villages. Various of those groups comprised larger social units denominated "pueblos". These in turn were organized in confederations under the authority of the more important chiefts. In the 1500's, after a process which included alliances based on intermarriages and wars of expansion, the greater part of the Muisca population had fallen under the domination of four great confederations: Bogotá (which dominated the great Sabana of Bogotá and neighboring areas), Tunja, Sogamoso, and Duitama, located in today's Department of Boyacá .

Guane double vessel

The Muisca economy was based, as we have described for Tairona and groups of Andes from Nariño, on vertically organized agriculture, which simultaneously employed diverse altitudes. The greater share of the villages were located in the cold valleys, at an average altitude of 2500 meters above sea level, lands whose fertility and average humidity permitted an extraordinary development of maize agriculture and the cultivation of roots common to the higher regions, fundamentally potatoes. Concurrently, the population exercised control over fields located in even colder regions and on the warmer, temperate slopes of the Eastern Cordillera. In this way, each family could, in many cases, have access to fields of coca, cotton, fruit trees, maize, manioc, and potatoes.

Among the Muiscas we find notable development in regional specialization. There were populations, such as Rá quira, whose expertise lay in producing ceramic vessels.

SUMMARY

MUISCA

700 A.D. - 1600 A.D.

Maize agricultural society characterized by marked social complexity. Economy based on vertically organized agriculture distributed over various altitudes and on the production of ceramics, goldwork, and textiles. Trade with lowlands.

GOLDWORKING

Pieces cast in the lost wax process, generally of tumbaga. Tunjos or figurative offerings, bird-shaped pendants, nose rings, and pectorals were produced. The use of molds permitted serial production of metal adornments. Guatavita, Pasca, and Ganchancip stand out as specialized goldworking centers.

Muisca "Tunjo" or votive figure. The goldwork from the high plains is very rich in representations of political, religious, and military leaders.

Other villages distinguished themselves by producing textiles, stone adornments, basketry, salt, fish or hallucinogenic drugs. All of this triggered the establishment of complex trade networks where the most important chiefs controlled the distribution of regional surpluses. A considerable portion of these surpluses were put into circulation and found their way to distant groups. The Muiscas, in fact, supplied textiles, gold, and emeralds to communities living on the Eastern Plains and, in the Magdalena River Valley.

Muisca goldwork can be divided into two phases of development. The first is represented by a series of objects found on the western flank of the mountain range, which consists of anthropomorphic figures, nose rings, representations of animals with raised tails, and a further series of articles produced in gold or tumbaga very similar to those from the Quimbaya Classic period. Later, after 1000 A.D., Muisca goldwork continued to develop until the arrival of Spaniards in the 1500's.

Goldwork production from the 1500's is a good example of the complexity of the distribution and exchange systems developed by the Muiscas. In all likelihood, copper deposits in the territory were mined. Nonetheless, all of the gold worked by the Muiscas came from outside territories, especially from the Magdalena valley. Even so, the Muiscas developed specialized centers to work the metals: places such as Guatavita, Gachancipá, and Pasca. Necklace beads, pectorals, diadems, ear ornaments, and nose rings usually cast using the lost wax process, the beeswax for which they acquired trading with groups from the Eastern Plains, were produced in many places and in sufficient quantity so as to supply both local and outside demands.

Among the Muiscas, the work of smelting and casting was performed under the supervision of priests or "chuques" who, after consuming narcotic drugs, would offer the pieces to their deities in sanctuaries. Normally, each offering was comprised of a group of pieces, not necessarily made of gold, in which the same basic idea,

Muisca "Eagle" discovered in Guatavita

associated with a specific petition, would be reproduced. Frequently, the offerings were deposited in ceramic vessels made to represent chiefs or shamans. Special petitions referred to agricultural calendar holidays, the installation of new chiefts or ceremonies prior to joining battle with enemy communities.

A large portion of Muisca goldwork production was oriented toward producing tunjos or offerings that represented different aspects of communal life: warriors, priests, chiefs, miniature villages, scenes depicting sacrifices, snakes, felines, miniature vessels, and baskets, among many other items. These pieces are very characteristic of the Muisca territory. A great variety of body ornaments such as bird-shaped pendants ("eagles"), circular shaped embossed pectorals, and diverse types of nose rings appear to be very similar to those made in the Sierra Nevada de Santa Marta, in the Sinú and Quimbaya areas, and in Central America, in the centuries immediately prior to the 1500's.

Muisca "eagle"

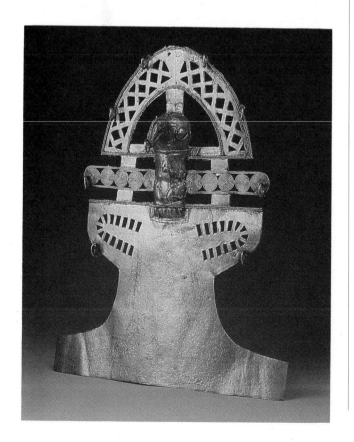

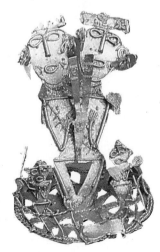

Representations of a Muisca "Fenced in" or village with important personages. Carmen de Carupá , Department of Cundinamarca.

Conclusions

In describing the goldworking developments of prehispanic Colombia, we have deciphered coherent patterns that permit the establishment of a clear relationship between the working of metals and the economic and political organization of the goldworking chiefdoms. The earliest goldwork is characterized by an emphasis on hammering techniques for pure gold. Great, spectacular pieces were produced, but not in large quantities. Later, complex cacicazgos emphasized smelting techniques, the employment of alloys and - above all - the serial production of cast pieces. Relatively speaking, the objects produced in later eras are less splendid than the enthralling ornaments of pure gold created by hammering. However, this does not indicate the slightest "degeneration" in goldworking. To the contrary, it denotes the development of different production strategies, linked to providing larger quantities of objects to a greater number of people.

The most ancient goldworking centers in the country are those in the south and southwest regions. There, we find the oldest evidence of social complexity concurrent with the elaboration of spectacular pieces of pure gold. The political nature of these first chiefdoms gave great importance to the exhibition of objects of prestige.

The metallic adornments that the chieftains wore required an enormous investment of work, and pieces were created to be splendid. During this era, which in general terms lasted from several centuries prior to and five or six hundred years into the our era, the populations in the south of the country also placed enormous emphasis on monumental statuary, networks of ceremonial pathways and also spectacular ceramics.

As the internal dynamics of development reached the southernmost parts of the country, the chiefdoms of the north developed their own goldwork. Initially, northern societies - Muisca, Sinú, and Tairona - copied Quimbaya Classic pieces, the first culture to emphasize casting using the lost wax process. The reason the pieces copied from the Quimbaya Classic style were popular is not clear. Probably, trade played an important role. As we have seen, each community autonomously solved its basic needs by controlling different ecosistems. Thus, trade was directed not so much toward supplying goods basic for survival but rather toward providing communities with prestige items which were exhibited by chiefs and shamans to emphasize their status. Probably Quimbaya Classic adornments circulated to the chiefdoms in the north of the country where, eventually, they were copied by local artisans. This process does not imply that the different societies from the north of the country shared linguistic, ethnic, or cultural ties. with those of the south They were societies that participated in networks of exchange and for which the acquisition and, ideally, the production of metal adornments were important.

With the development of complex chiefdoms in the north, particularly on the high plains of Cundinamarca and Boyacá and in the Sierra Nevada de Santa Marta, goldwork was completely transformed. It should be observed that goldwork was produced in specialized centers, that there was greater emphasis placed on the utilization of tumbaga and even molds for serial production. This body of evidence indicates that goldwork was oriented not toward the production of exclusive pieces but rather toward large quantities of articles which required less production time per unit. The emergence of specialized goldworking centers in Tairona (Bondigua), Sinú, Quimbaya (Dabeiba), and Muisca (Guatavita, Gachancipá and Pasca) freed artisans who worked gold from other duties within the society. The use of tumbaga to reduce the point of fusion of the metals translated into tremendous savings in time and resources, variables which are particularly critical when the goal is to produce a considerable quantity of items. While the display of a few impressive adornments was crucial for maintaining status in early southern chiefdoms, more direct control over the mining, production and circulation of less impressive adornments predominated in the more advanced chiefdoms that the

Spaniards found at the time of conquest. Thus, instead of a decline in goldworking processes, we witness notable progress in artisan and technical specialization.

Goldworking practices are essentially the result of the long structuring process belonging to complex societies. As can be inferred from our thesis, none of the pieces on display at the Museo del Oro can be separated from the social and economic nature of the society that produced them. Clearly, archaeologists cannot place the economic production and social organization next to each piece within the showcase. In the majority of cases, we must accept the selection of certain artifacts as representative of a whole body of work, those which are the most spectacular.

However, more than pieces of jewelry or adornments, they are the result of a process of a particular history which includes, precisely, economic and political variables.

We know more about the goldworking societies today than we did in the past, a knowledge based on many things other than the addition of new spectacular gold pieces. The metal adornments displayed in showcases and those which are not sufficiently attractive to be displayed are part of a vaster universe, composed of economic, cultural and political variables that wrought social change.

Thus, when visiting the museum, it is worth your while to remember that the history of goldword in Colombia is inseparable from that of the peoples who were nurtured by it.

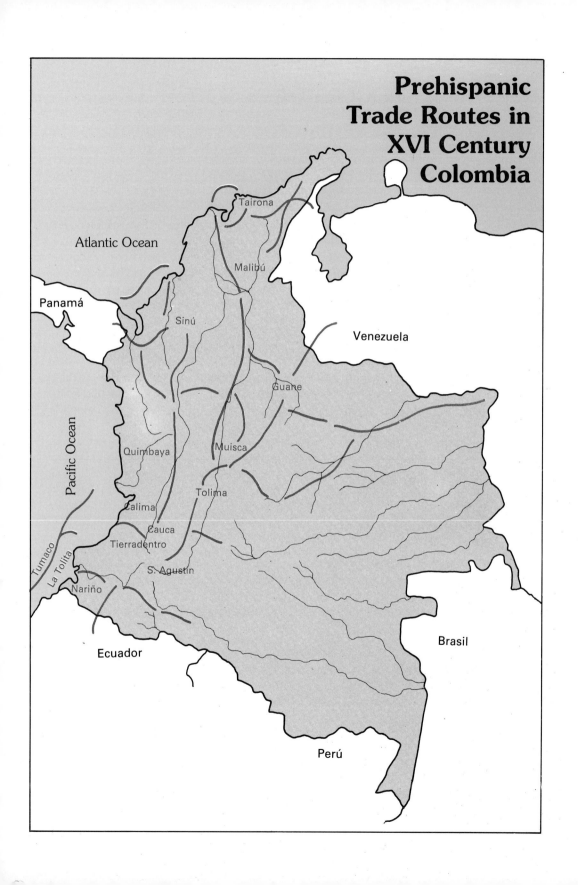

Prehispanic Trade Routes in XVI Century Colombia

Atlantic Ocean

Panamá

Venezuela

Pacific Ocean

Tairona

Malibú

Sinú

Guane

Quimbaya

Muisca

Tolima

Calima

Cauca

Tierradentro

Tumaco

La Tolita

Nariño

S. Agustín

Brasil

Ecuador

Perú

BIBLIOGRAPHICAL NOTES

1- Several works treat the subject of prehispanic goldwork. The following are recommended: "Precolumbian Gold", written by Julie Jones and published in El Dorado - The Gold of Ancient Colombia, American Federation of Arts, 1984; Sweat of the Sun, Tears of the Moon - Gold and Silver in Pre-columbian Art, by André Emmerich, Hacker Art Books, New York, 1984; "Notas históricas sobre la orfebrería prehisp nica en Colombia", by Luis Duque, Homenaje al profesor Paul Rivet, I.C.A.N., 1958; La Orfebrería Prehisp nica de Colombia, by Ana María Falchetti and Clemencia Plazas, Museo del Oro, 1983; and Gold of El Dorado, by Warwick Bray, Royal Academy, London, 1978. A complete catalog of the pieces in the Museum's collection was published between 1953 and 1958 by José Pérez de Barradas, Banco de la República.

2- Concerning technological aspects, consult: "Orfebrería chibcha y su definición científica", by A. Barriga, Revista de la Academia de Ciencias, 11(42), 1961, Bogotá and "Precolumbian Metalwork in Colombia and its Neighbors", by W. Root, in Essays in Precolumbian Art and Archaeology, Harvard University Press, 1964. Works which treat specific technological aspects have been published by Warwick Bray, David Scott, Karen Bruhns, and Clemencia Plazas. Concerning the interpretation of symbolism, see: "Andean Value Systems and the Development of Prehispanic Metallurgy", by Heather Lechtman, in Technology and Culture, 25(1), 1984; "Precious Metals and Politics: Style and Ideology in the Intermediate Area and Peru", by Mary Helms, in Journal of American Lore, number 7, volume 2, 1981, and, especially, Orfebrería y chamanismo: Estudio iconográfico del Museo del Oro, by Gerardo Reichel-Dolmatoff, Editorial Colina, 1988. Also recommended: "The Goldwork of Panama - An Iconographic and Chronological Perspective", by Richard Cooke in The Art of Precolumbian Gold - The Jan Michell Collection, Julie Jones Editor, 1985.

3- For historical aspects of the development of metallurgy in general and their relationship to social complexity, see: "Varna and the Emergence of Wealth in Europe", by Colin Renfrew, in The Social Life of Things, Cambridge University Press, 1988. Also recommended: "The Archaeological Interpretation of Prehistoric Metalworking", by Michael Rowlands, in World Archaeology, Volume 3, pp. 20-24, 1971.

4- This digest of the processes of prehispanic Colombian development is based on summaries written by Gerardo Reichel-Dolmatoff in Arqueología de Colombia - un texto introductorio, published by Fundación Segunda Expedición Bot nica, 1986 and by Warwick Bray in "Across the Darien Gap - A Colombian View of Isthmian Archaeology" in The Archaeology of Lower Central America, Albuquerque, 1984. In Colombia, studies on the hunting stages of societies have been carried out primarily by Gonzalo Correal; those concerning the cultivation of roots and the introduction of maize agriculture, by Gerardo Reichel-Dolmatoff and Carlos Angulo. In reference to the characteristics of mangrove economy, consult: "Life in the 'Garden of Eden' - Causes and Consequences of the Adoption of Marine Diets by Human Societies", by David Yesner, in Food and Evolution, M. Harris editor, published by University Press, Philadelphia, 1987.

Warwick Bray and other scholars, Like Ana María Falchetti and Clemencia Plazas, have helped to define the differences between the goldworking traditions of the northern and southern parts of the country. For further information, see Patrones culturales de la orfebrería prehispánica de Colombia by Ana María Falchetti and Clemencia Plazas, Banco de la República, 1986.

5. There is a very good brief summary on Calima: "El hombre y su medio ambiente en Calima", by Leonore Herrera, Marianne Cardale and Warwick Bray in Revista Colombiana de Antropología, Number 24, Bogot , 1984. Data on hunters/gatherers were obtained by the archaeologist, Héctor Salgado. For information on Calima goldwork, see: Orfebrería Prehisp nica de Colombia by José Pérez de Barradas, Banco de la República, 1958 and "Gold Objects from Primavera - Links Between Calima, San Agustín and the Cauca Valley" by Clemencia Plazas in Revista Procalima, number 3.

6- Concerning Tumaco archaeology, the following works are recommended: "Excavaciones arqueológicas en la región de Tumaco, Nariño, Colombia" by François Buchard in Revista Colombiana de Antropología, 24, 1983 and "Arqueología de la costa pacífica caucana", by Diógenes Patiño in Boletín de Arqueología, Banco de la República, 2(1), 1987. Concerning metallurgy, see: "Orfebrería prehisp nica de las llanuras del Pacífico del Ecuador y Colombia" by David Scott and François Buchard in Boletín Museo del Oro 22, 1988.

7- On San Agustín, see: Exploraciones arqueológicas en San Agustín, Alto los Idolos, montículos y tumbas by Luis Duque and Julio César Cubillos, Banco de la República, Bogot , 1979, and Contribuciones al conocimiento de la estratigrafía cerá0mica de San Agustín by Gerardo Reichel-Dolmatoff, Biblioteca Banco Popular, 1975. Recent investigations in San Agustín or neighboring areas have been carried out by archaeologists: Héctor Llanos, Robert Drennan, Anabella Dur n, Leonardo Moreno, Carlos S nchez, and Luis Salamanca, among others.

8- A good, general introductory account of Tierradentro can be found in: Tierradentro by Alvaro Cháves and Mauricio Puerta, El Ancora Ed., Bogot , 1986. The exploitation of salt in the region is described by Ana María Groot in "Excavaciones arqueológicas en Tierradentro" by Juan Yanguez in Revista Colombiana de Antropología, 15, Bogot , 1971. Other scholars who have done research and written on the area are Eliécer Silva Celis and José Pérez de Barradas.

9- For archaeology of the Cauca River area, consult: Arqueología del Valle del Cauca - asentamientos prehisp nicos en la suela planta del río Cauca by Julio César Cubillos, Banco de la República, 1984.

10- One of the few references on Tolima archaeology can be found in the article: "Arqueología de Rioblanco (Chaparral, Tolima)" by Julio César Cubillos in Boletín de Arqueología, 5(1), Bogotá. Also see: "Brigmosal: A Site Near El Guamo, Tolima" by Thomas Myers in Journal of the Steward Anthropological Society, 4(2), 1973. Ethnic historical data on the region is known thanks to the Spanish scholar, Manuel Lucena Samoral.

11- For information on the archaeology of Nariño, see: "Asentamientos prehispánicos en el Altiplano de Ipiales" by María Victoria Uribe in Revista Colombiana de Antropología, 21 Bogot . Concerning regional goldworking, see: "Orfebrería prehispánica del Altiplano Nariñense" by Clemencia Plazas in Revista Colombiana de Antropología, 21, 1979.

12- For Quimbaya, we recommend: "Stylistic Affinities Between the Quimbaya Gold Style and a Little-known Ceramic Style of the Middle Cauca Valley, Colombia, Ñapa Pacha, 8, The University of California at Berkeley, 1971, and Ancient Pottery of the Middle Cauca Valley", Colombia, Ann Arbor, Michigan, 1967 - both works by Karen Bruhns, and "Complejos arqueológicos y grupos étnicos del siglo XVI en el occidente de Antioquia", by Nayla Castillo in Boletín Museo del Oro, 20, 1988. The ethnic history of the region is known thanks to works such as: Señorío y Barbarie en el Valle del Cauca by Hermann Trimborn, Consejo Superior de Investigaciones Científicas, Madrid, 1949, Los quimbaya by Luis Duque, I.C.A.N., 1970, and Los quimbaya by Juan Friede, El Ancora Editores, Bogot, 1982. On relationships between periods of early occupation and Yotoco: "Notas sobre una tumba de cancel hallada en el municipio de Dosquebradas, Risaralda - orfebrería de la tradición metalúrgica del suroccidente hallada en el Cauca Medio" by Marianne Cardale, Sory Morales and Oscar Osorio in Boletín Museo del Oro, 22, 1988. Archaeologists interested in the area and who are currently working on projects include Cristina Moreno, Camilo Rodríguez, and Gonzalo Jaramillo.

13- For the lower San Jorge region, the primary bibliographic reference is: Asentamientos prehispánicos en el Bajo San Jorge, Banco de la República, 1982. other articles on goldworks of the region were written by the same authors who wrote the above general essay. Ann Legast authored a notable work on regional goldworking entitled: La fauna en la orfebrería Sinú published by Banco de la República, 1985.

14- For studies on the prehispanic development of the Sierra Nevada de Santa Marta, see: Buritica Ceramic Chronology: A Seriation from the Tairona Area, Colombia, by Jack Wynn, Doctoral Thesis, University of Missouri, 1975; "Contribuciones a la cronología de la cultura tairona", by Henning Bischof as published in "Cartas del 38 Congreso Internacional de Americanistas", Munich, 1968; y "Contribución a la periodización cultural en el litoral del Parque Tairona" by Augusto Oyuela, Boletín de Arqueología, 1(1), Banco de la República, Bogotá, 1987. As regards the ethnic history of the region, the following work is recommended: Datos histórico-culturales sobre las tribus de la antigua Gobernación de Santa Marta by Gerardo Reichel-Dolmatoff, Instituto Etnológico del Magdalena, 1951. A detailed study of the development of Nequanje goldworking "Das Gold von Tairona: Entwicklung und Kultur-historischer Kontext" was written by Ana María Falchetti in "Tairona Goldschmiede der Sierra Nevada de Santa Marta, Kolumbien", Escala, Bogotá, 1986. Concerning the uses of thermal floors, see: "Algunos aspectos de la economía tairona en el litoral adyacente a Ciénaga (Magdalena)", by Carl Langebaek in Manguaré, 4, 1987.

15- Information relevant to the developments of groups that inhabited the high plains of Cundinamarca and Boyac before the Muisca society was derived primarily from works by Marianne Cardale, particularly: Las salinas de Zipaquirá su explotación indígena, Banco de la República, 1981. Outstanding works on the Muisca period are: Arqueología de Tunja by Neyla Castillo, Banco de la República, 1984, and Arqueología de Sutamarch n by Ana María Falchetti, Banco Popular, 1975. On ethnic history and economic organization, see: Los chibchas - organización sociopolítica by Sylvia Broadbent, Serie Latinoamericana, 5, Universidad Nacional de Colombia, 1964 and Mercados, poblamiento e integración étnica entre los Muiscas en el siglo XVI by Carl Langebaek, Banco de la República, 1987. Regarding Muisca goldworking, consult Clemencia Plazas: Nueva motodología para la clasificación de la orfebrería precolombina, Plazas Ed., 1975.

16- Much ethnographic evidence suggests that the acquisition of luxury items produced by more complex societies was fostered by local political leaders to reinforce their prestige These items were copied locally, reproducing the same shapes and elements of decoration, despite the fact that there were no cultural ties with the society that had originally produced those articles. For example, see: "The Olmec and The Valley of Oaxaca: A Model for Inter-regional Interaction in Formative Times" by Kent Flannery in Dumbarton Oake Conference on Olmec, Washington, 1968. A similar stand, but one which overemphasizes the circulation of items and minimizes the capacity of different societies to develop their own practices is: Ancient Panama - Chiefs in Search of Power by Mary Helms, University of Texas Press, 1979. This book contains valuable data on the role of goldworks as status and prestige symbols for prehispanic chieftains.